How to Obtain

FULLNESS OF POWER

In Christian Life and Service

By R. A. TORREY

Author of

What the Bible Teaches, How to Work for Christ,
How to Pray, The Holy Spirit: Who He Is,
and What He Does, etc.

"God hath spoken once; twice have I heard this;
that power belongeth unto God."—Psa. 62:11.

"Be strong in the Lord, and in the power of his
might."—Eph. 6:10.

"Ye are strong, and the word of God abideth in
you."—I John 2:14.

"Strengthened with power through his Spirit in
the inward man."—Eph. 3:16, R.V.

SWORD of the LORD
PUBLISHERS
P.O.BOX 1099, MURFREESBORO, TN 37133

Copyright 1897, by
FLEMING H. REVELL COMPANY

*This edition published by SWORD OF THE LORD PUBLISHERS,
Murfreesboro, Tennessee, by agreement with Fleming H. Revell*

ISBN 0-87398-368-8

Printed in the U.S.A.

AUTHOR'S PREFACE

From many earnest hearts there is rising a cry for more power: more power in our personal conflict with the world, the flesh, and the Devil; more power in our work for others. The Bible makes the way to obtain this longed-for power very plain. There is no presumption in undertaking to tell "How to Obtain Fullness of Power in Christian Life and Service"; for the Bible itself tells, and the Bible was intended to be understood. The Bible statement of the way is not mystical nor mysterious; it is very plain and straightforward. If we will only make personal trial of "The Power of the Word of God," "The Power of the Blood of Christ," "The Power of the Holy Spirit," "The Power of Prayer," "The Power of a Surrendered Life," we will then know "The Fullness of Power in Christian Life and Service." We will try to make this plain in the following chapters.

The present volume has been written partly in response to a request from some who have used the author's book, *How to Bring Men to Christ*, that he would write another book for use in the training of those who have come to Christ. But the book has also another and far more important purpose. There are many who do not even know that there is a life of abiding rest, joy, satisfaction, and power; and many others who, while they think there must be something beyond the life they know, are in ignorance as to how to obtain it. This book is written to help them.

CONTENTS

5

CHAPTER I

The Power of the Word of God

"*POWER BELONGETH unto God.*"—Psa. 62:11. The great reservoir of the power that belongs to God is His own Word—the Bible. If we wish to make it ours, we must go to that Book. Yet people abound in the church who are praying for power and neglecting the Bible. Men are longing to have power for fruit-bearing in their own lives and yet forget that Jesus has said: "The seed is the word of God" (Luke 8:11). They are longing to have power to melt the cold heart and break the stubborn will, and yet forget that God has said: "Is not my word like as a fire? . . . and like a hammer that breaketh the rock in pieces?" (Jer. 23:29). If we are to obtain fullness of power in life and service, we must feed upon the Word of God. There is no other food so strengthening. If we will not take time to study the Bible, we cannot have power, any more than we can have physical power if we will not take time to eat nutritious food.

Let us see what the Word of God has power to do.

1. First of all, the Word of God has power to convict of sin. In Acts 2:37 we read,

> "*Now when they heard this, they were pricked in their heart, and said unto Peter and to the rest of the apostles, Men and brethren, what shall we do?*"

If we look back and see what it was they heard and that produced this deep conviction, we find that it was simply the Word of God. If you will read Peter's sermon, you will find it one of the most biblical sermons ever preached. It was Scripture from beginning to end. It was, then, the Word of God, carried home by the Spirit of God, that pricked them to their heart. If you wish to produce conviction, you must give men the Word of God. I heard a man pray some time ago this prayer, "O God, convict us of sin," a very good prayer, but unless you bring your soul in contact with that instrument which God has appointed for the conviction of sin, you will not have conviction of sin. If you wish to produce conviction in others, you must use the Word to do it.

Not long ago a fine-looking young man came into our inquiry-room. I said to him: "Are you a Christian?"

"No, sir."

"Why not?"

"I think Christianity is a first-rate thing, but I have not much feeling about this."

"But," I said, "do you not know that you are a sinner?"

He said: "Yes, sir, I suppose I am; but I am not very much of a sinner. I am a pretty good sort of a fellow."

I replied: "So, my friend, you have not very much conviction of sin. I have something in my hand that is a divinely-appointed instrument to produce conviction of sin." I opened my Bible to Matthew 22:37, 38 and asked him to read it. He read, "Thou shalt love the Lord thy God with all thy heart, and with all thy soul, and with all thy mind. This is the first and great commandment."

"What commandment is that?" I asked.

He replied: "The first and great commandment."

"In the light of that, what must be the first and great sin?"

He replied: "It must be to neglect to keep that commandment."

"Have you kept it?"

The Spirit of God took it home to his heart then and there. It was not long before we were kneeling, and he was asking God for mercy through Christ.

2. In the next place, the Word of God has power to regenerate. In I Peter 1:23 we read,

> *"Being born again, not of corruptible seed, but of incorruptible, by the word of God, which liveth and abideth for ever."*

In James 1:18 we read,

> *"Of his own will begat he us with the word of truth, that we should be a kind of firstfruits of his creatures."*

If you wish to be born again, the way is very simple. Take the Word of God concerning Christ crucified and risen, and drop it into your heart by meditation upon it. Look to God by His Holy Spirit to quicken it, believe it with the heart, and the work is done. If you wish to see someone else born again, give him the Word of God. The process of regeneration on our side is the simplest thing in the world. On God's side it is mysterious, but with that we have nothing to do. The process is simply this: the human heart is the soil; you and I are sowers; the Word of God is the seed which we drop into that soil. God quickens it by His Holy Spirit and gives the increase (I Cor. 3:6). The heart closes around the Word by faith, and the new life is the product. The new birth is simply the impartation of a new nature, the impartation of God's nature.

But how are we made partakers of God's nature? Read II Peter 1:4 (R.V.) and the context: "That through these [exceeding great and precious promises] ye may become partakers of the divine nature." That is all there is to it. The Word of God is the seed out of which the divine nature springs up in the human soul.

3. Again, the Word of God has power to produce faith. In Romans 10:17 we read,

> *"So then faith cometh by hearing, and hearing by the word of God."*

You can never get faith by merely praying; you can never get it by any effort of the will; you can never get it by trying to pump it up in any way. Faith is the product of a certain cause, and that cause is the Word of God. It is so, for example, with saving faith. Suppose you want a man to have saving faith. Simply give him something definite from God's Word upon which he can rest. The Philippian jailer asked, "Sirs, what must I do to be saved?" (Acts 16:30), and Paul answered, "Believe on the Lord Jesus Christ, and thou shalt be saved, and thy house" (Acts 16:31). But Paul did not stop there. Read verse 32, "And they spake unto him the word of the Lord, and to all that were in his house." They did not merely tell the Philippian jailer to believe on the Lord Jesus Christ, and then leave him there floundering in the dark without giving him something to believe, or something for his faith to rest upon. They gave that which God has ordained to produce faith.

It is at this point that we often make a mistake. We tell people, "Believe, believe, believe," but do not show them how, do not give them anything definite to believe. The biblical way and the intelligent way is, when you tell a man to believe, to give him something to believe. Give him, for example, Isaiah 53:6, and thus hold up Christ crucified; or, give him I Peter 2:24. Here he has something for his faith to rest upon. Faith must have a foundation. Faith cannot float in thin air. It is pitiable to see men told to believe, to believe, to believe— and then give nothing to rest their faith upon.

Not only saving faith comes through the Word of God, but prevailing faith in prayer does also. Suppose I read Mark 11:

24, "What things soever ye desire, when ye pray, believe that ye receive them, and ye shall have them." I used to say, "The way to get anything I want is to believe I am going to get it." I would kneel down and pray and try to believe, but I did not get the things that I asked for. I had no real faith. Real faith must have a warrant. Before I can truly believe I am to receive what I ask, I must have a definite promise of God's Word, or a definite leading of the Holy Spirit, to rest my faith upon.

What, then, shall we do? We come into God's presence. There is something we desire. Now the question is, Is there any promise in God's Word regarding this which we desire? We look into the Word of God and find the promise. All we have to do is to spread that promise out before God. For example, we say: "Heavenly Father, we desire the Holy Spirit. Thou hast said in Thy Word, 'If ye then, being evil, know how to give good gifts unto your children: how much more shall your heavenly Father give the Holy Spirit to them that ask him?' And Thou hast said again in Acts 2:39 that 'the promise is unto you, and to your children, and to all that are afar off, even as many as the Lord our God shall call.' I am a called man; I am a saved man. And here I have Your word for it. You have promised it. I ask Thee now to fill me with the Holy Spirit." We then take I John 5:14, 15, and say, "Father, this is the confidence I have in Thee, that, if I ask anything according to Thy will—and I know that this is according to Thy will—Thou hearest me, and, if I know that Thou hearest me, I know that I have the petition that I have asked of Thee." Then I rise up, standing upon this promise of God, and say, "It is mine." And it will be mine. The only way to have a faith that prevails in prayer is to study your Bible, and know the promises, and lay them before God when you pray. George Mueller is one of the mightiest men of prayer in this century. But he always prepares for prayer by studying the Word (John 15:7).

It is just the same with the faith that we desire instead of doubt. This also comes by the Word of God. Suppose you have a skeptic to deal with, and you wish that man to have faith. What will you do with him? Give him a book on Christian evidences? I have nothing to say against books on Christian evidences. But there is an inspired Book on Christian evidences, and it is worth all the libraries ever written on this subject. Turn to John 20:31, "But these are written, that ye might believe that Jesus is the Christ, the Son of God; and that believing ye might have life through his name." Clearly, then, this Book of John was given that, through what is "written" therein, men "might believe that Jesus is the Christ, the Son of God; and that believing they might have life through his name." The Gospel of John is an inspired book on Christian evidences. What, then, shall we do with ourselves if we are skeptics? What shall we do with others? First, find out whether their will is surrendered or not. "If any man willeth to do his will, he shall know of the teaching, whether it is of God, or whether I speak from myself" (John 7:17, R.V.). After the will is surrendered, just say, "Take this book and read it thoughtfully and honestly and come back and tell me the result." The result is absolutely sure.

There is no man, agnostic, infidel, or whatever you please, whose will is surrendered to the truth, who will take this Book to God and ask Him to give him light, who will not come out believing in Jesus as the Christ, the Son of God. I have tried this with I know not how many men and women, and there has never been one exception to the rule laid down by Christ. It has always come out the same way.

The faith that gets the victory over the world, the flesh, and the Devil; the faith that wins mighty victories for God, is also through the Word. (I John 5:4; Eph. 6:16; Heb. 11:33, 34).

Very early in my ministry I read a sermon by Mr. Moody. In it there was something to the effect that a man would not amount to anything if he had not faith. I said, "That sermon is true. I must have faith." I went to work and tried to work up faith. I did not succeed a bit. The more I tried to work up faith, the less I had. But one day I ran across this text, "So then faith cometh by hearing, and hearing by the word of God" (Rom. 10:17), and I had learned the great secret of faith, one of the greatest secrets I have ever learned. I commenced to feed my faith on the Word of God; and as I have thus fed it, it has kept on growing from that day to this. So in every aspect we see that faith cometh by hearing, and hearing by the Word of God. If we are to have faith—and if we are to have power for God, we must have faith—we must feed steadily, largely, daily upon the Word of God.

4. In the next place, the Word of God has power to cleanse. In Ephesians 5:25, 26, we read,

"Husbands, love your wives, even as Christ also loved the church, and gave himself for it; that he might sanctify and cleanse it with the washing of water by the word."

The Word of God has power not only to take impurity out of the heart, but to cleanse the outward life as well. If you wish a clean outward life, you must wash often by bringing your life in contact with the Word of God. If one lives in a city whose atmosphere is polluted with smoke, when he goes into the street his hands will become black. He must wash frequently if he wishes to keep clean. We all live in a world whose atmosphere is polluted, a very dirty world. As we go out from day to day and come in contact with this dirty world, there is absolutely only one way to keep clean, and that is by taking frequent baths in the Word of God. You must bathe every day, and take plenty of time to do it. A daily, prolonged, thoughtful bath in the Word of God is the only thing that will keep a life clean (Psa. 119:9).

5. In the next place, the Word of God has power to build up. In Acts 20:32 we read,

> *"I commend you to God, and to the word of his grace, which is able to build you up."*

We hear a great deal in these days about character-building. The Word of God is that by which we must carry it on if it is to be done right. In II Peter 1:5-7 we have a picture of a seven-story-and-basement Christian. The great trouble today is we have so many one-story Christians, and the reason is neglect of the Word.

In I Peter 2:2 we have a similar thought expressed under a different figure, "As newborn babes, desire the sincere milk of the word, that ye may grow thereby." If we are to grow, we must have wholesome, nutritious food and plenty of it. The only spiritual food that contains all the elements necessary for symmetrical Christian growth is the Word of God. A Christian can no more grow as he ought without feeding frequently, regularly, and largely upon the Word of God, than a baby can grow as he ought without proper nutriment.

6. In the next place, the Word of God has power to make wise. Psalm 119:130 is worthy of the most careful attention,

> *"The entrance of thy words giveth light; it giveth understanding unto the simple."*

There is more wisdom in the Bible than there is in all the other literature of the ages. The one who studies the Bible, if he does not study any other book, will know more of real wisdom—wisdom that counts for eternity as well as time, wisdom that this perishing world needs to know, wisdom for which hungry hearts are starving today—than the man who reads every other book and neglects his Bible. The man who studies the Bible and neglects all other books will be wiser than the man who studies all other books and neglects the Bible. The man who studies the Bible will have more to say that is worth saying, and that wise people wish to hear, than any man who studies everything else and neglects the one Book.

This has been illustrated over and over again in the history of the church. The men who have greatly affected the spiritual history of this world, the men who have brought about great reformations in morals and doctrine, the men whom others have flocked to hear and upon whose words people have hung, have been Bible men in every instance, and in many cases they knew little beside the Bible. I have seen men and women without culture, who have had almost no advantages in school, but who knew their Bibles; and I would rather sit at their feet and learn the wisdom that falls from their lips, than listen to the man who knows much about philosophy and science and theology even, and does not know anything about the Word of God. There is wonderful force in the words of Paul to Timothy, "All scripture is given by inspiration of God, and is profitable for doctrine, for reproof, for correction, for instruction in righteousness: That the man of God may be perfect, throughly [the Revised Version says "completely"] furnished unto all good works" (II Tim. 3:16, 17). Through what? Through the study of the Book.

7. The Word of God has power to give assurance of eternal life. In I John 5:13, R.V., we read,

"These things have I written unto you, that ye may know that ye have eternal life, even unto you that believe on the name of the Son of God."

That is, the assurance of eternal life comes through what is "written." Suppose one has not assurance of salvation, what shall we do? Tell him to pray until he gets it? Not at all. Take him to some such passage as John 3:36: "He that believeth on the Son hath everlasting life." Hold him right to that point until he takes God's Word for it, and then is sure that he has everlasting life because he believes on the Son, and because God says that "he that believeth on the Son HATH everlasting life."

8. The Word of God has power to bring peace into the heart. In Psalm 85:8 we read,

"I will hear what God the Lord will speak: for he will speak peace unto his people, and to his saints."

There are many people looking for peace today, longing for peace, praying for peace. But deep peace of heart comes from the study of the Word of God. There is, for example, one passage in the Bible which, if we feed upon it daily until it really gets into our hearts and gets hold of us, will banish all anxiety forever. It is Romans 8:28, "And we know that all things work together for good to them that love God, to them who are the called according to his purpose." Nothing can come to us that is not one of the "all things." If we really believe this passage, and it really takes hold upon us, whatever comes, it will not disturb our peace.

9. The Word of God has power to produce joy. Jeremiah says in chapter 15, verse 16,

"Thy words were found, and I did eat them; and thy word was unto me the joy and rejoicing of mine heart."

And Jesus said in John 15:11,

"These things have I spoken unto you, that my joy might remain in you, and that your joy might be full."

Clearly, then, fullness of joy comes through the Word of God. There is no joy on this earth from any worldly source like the joy that kindles and glows in the heart of a believer in Jesus Christ as he feeds upon the Word of God, and as the Word of God is brought home to his heart by the power of the Holy Spirit.

10. Patience, comfort, and hope also come through the Word of God. Romans 15:4,

"For whatsoever things were written aforetime were written for our learning, that we through patience and comfort of the scriptures might have hope."

11. Finally, the Word of God has power to protect from error and sin. In Acts 20:29-32, the Apostle Paul warned the elders at Ephesus of the errors that would creep in among them, and he commended them, in closing, "to God and to the word of his grace." In a similar way, Paul, writing to Timothy, the bishop of the same church, said:

"But evil men and seducers shall wax worse and worse, deceiving, and being deceived. But continue thou in the things which thou hast learned and hast been assured of, knowing of whom thou hast learned them; And that from a child thou hast known the holy scriptures, which are able to make thee wise unto salvation through faith which is in Christ Jesus."—II Tim. 3:13-15.

The one who feeds constantly on the Word of God is proof against the multiplying errors of the day. It is simple neglect of the Word that has left so many a prey to the many false doctrines that the Devil, in his subtlety, is endeavoring to insinuate into the church of Christ today. And the Word of God has not only power to protect from error, but from sin as well. In Psalm 119:11 we read: "Thy word have I hid in mine heart, that I might not sin against thee." The man who feeds daily on the Word of God will be proof against the temptations of the Devil. Any day we neglect to feed on the Word of God, we leave an open door through which Satan is sure to enter into our hearts and lives. Even the Son of God Himself met and overcame the temptations of the adversary by the Scriptures. To each of Satan's temptations, He replied,

"It is written" (Matt. 4:4, 7, 10). Satan left the field completely vanquished.

It is evident from what has been said that the first step toward obtaining fullness of power in Christian life and service is the study of the Word. There can be no fullness of power in life and service if the Bible is neglected. In much that is now written on power, also in much that is said in conventions, this fact is overlooked. The work of the Holy Spirit is magnified, but the instrument through which the Holy Spirit works is largely forgotten. The result is transient enthusiasm and activity, but no steady continuance and increase in power and usefulness.

We cannot obtain power, and we cannot maintain power, in our own lives, and in our work for others, unless there is deep and frequent meditation upon the Word of God. If our leaf is not to wither and whatsoever we do is to prosper, our delight must be in the law of the Lord and we must meditate therein day and night (Psa. 1:2, 3). Of course, it is much easier, and therefore much more agreeable to our spiritual laziness, to go to a convention or revival meeting, and claim a "filling with the Holy Spirit," than it is to peg along day after day, month after month, year after year, digging into the Word of God. But a "filling with the Spirit" that is not maintained by persistent study of the Word will soon vanish. It is well to bear in mind that precisely the results which Paul in one place ascribes to being "filled with the Spirit" (Eph. 5:18-22), he in another place ascribes to letting "the word of Christ dwell in you richly" (Col. 3:16-18). Evidently Paul knew of no filling with the Holy Spirit divorced from deep and constant meditation upon the Word. To sum all up, anyone who wishes to obtain and maintain fullness of power in Christian life and service must feed constantly upon the Word of God.

CHAPTER II

The Power of the Blood
of Christ

"*POWER BELONGETH unto God.*" It is therefore at man's disposal. But there is one thing that separates between man and God, that is, sin. We read in Isaiah, "Behold, the Lord's hand is not shortened, that it cannot save; neither his ear heavy, that it cannot hear: But your iniquities have separated between you and your God, and your sins have hid his face from you, that he will not hear" (Isa. 59:1, 2). Before we can know God's power in our lives and service, sin must be put away from between God and us. It is the blood that puts away sin (Heb. 9:26). We must know the power of the blood if we are to know the power of God. Our knowing experimentally the power of the Word, the power of the Holy Spirit, and the power of prayer, is dependent upon our knowing the power of the blood of Christ. Let us see what the blood of Christ has power to do:

1. First of all, the blood of Christ is a propitiation for sin. In Romans 3:25, R.V., we read,

"Whom God set forth to be a propitiation, through faith, in his blood, to show his righteousness because of the passing over of the sins done aforetime, in the forbearance of God."

In the earlier verses of this chapter Paul has proven all men to be sinners, "every mouth is stopped," all the world is seen to be "guilty before God." But God is holy, a God who hates sin. God's hatred of sin is no play hatred. It is real, it is living, it is active. It must make itself manifest somehow. God's wrath at sin must strike somewhere. What hope then is there for any of us; for we "all have sinned, and come short of the glory of God"? In verse 25, God gives us His own answer to this tremendously-important question. There is hope for us because God Himself has provided a propitiation, the shed blood of Christ. God has 'set forth Christ to be a propitiation, through faith, by his blood.' The wrath of God at sin strikes on Him instead of striking on us. Of this great truth the Prophet Isaiah got a glimpse several hundred years before the birth of Christ. "All we like sheep have gone astray; we have turned every one to his own way; and the Lord hath laid [literally, made to strike] on him the iniquity of us all" (Isa. 53:6).

The first power of Christ's blood is as a propitiation for sin, affording a mark for and satisfying God's holy wrath at sin. He is "our passover" (I Cor. 5:7) and when God sees His blood, He will pass over and spare us, sinners though we are. (Compare Exod. 12:13, 23.)

This propitiation is chiefly for the believer, "a propitiation, through faith." All of God's wrath at the believer's sins is fully appeased or satisfied in the blood of Christ. What a wonderfully comforting thought it is, when we think how often and how greatly we have sinned, and then think how infinitely holy God is, how He hates sin, to think that God's wrath has already been fully appeased in the shed blood of His own Son, the propitiation which He Himself provided!

The blood of Christ in a certain measure avails for all, for unbelievers as well as for believers, for the vilest sinner and the most stubborn unbeliever and blasphemer. In I John 2:2,

R.V., we read, "And he is the propitiation for our sins; and not for ours only, but also for the whole world." By the shed blood of Christ a basis is provided upon which God can deal in mercy with the whole world. All of God's dealings in mercy with man are on the ground of the shed blood of Christ. God's dealings with those who ridicule the doctrine of the Atonement, God's dealings with Voltaire, Tom Paine and Colonel Ingersoll, are all on the ground of that shed blood. All of God's dealings in mercy with any man since the fall of Adam are on the ground of that shed blood. If it had not been for the shed blood, God could never have dealt in mercy with a sinner, but must have at once cut him off in his sin.

If anyone asks, How then could God have dealt in mercy with sinners before Christ came and died?—the answer is simple. Jesus is the Lamb that hath been "slain from the foundation of the world" (Rev. 13:8). From the moment sin entered into the world, God had His eyes upon that sacrifice which He Himself had prepared from the foundation of the world. And in the very Garden of Eden the blood of sacrifices that pointed forward as types to the true sacrifice began to flow. It is the power of the blood which has secured to men all the merciful things God has wrought for them since sin entered. The most determined rejector of Christ owes all he has that is good to the blood of Christ.

2. Again in Ephesians 1:7, R.V., we read,

"... We have our redemption through his blood, the forgiveness of our trespasses. ..."

Through the blood of Christ we have our redemption, the forgiveness of sins. Forgiveness of sin is not something the believer in Christ is to look for in the future; it is something he already has. "We *have*," says Paul, "the forgiveness of our trespasses." The forgiveness of sin is not something we are to do something to secure. It is something which the blood of

Christ has already secured, and which our faith simply appropriates and enjoys. Forgiveness has already been secured for every believer in Christ by the power of the blood.

You have heard of the old woman who lay dying. Her rector heard of it and called upon her. "They tell me," he said, "that you are dying."

"Yes," she replied.

"And have you made your peace with God?"

"No," came the answer.

"And are you not afraid to meet God without making your peace with Him?"

"Not at all," was the answer that startled the minister.

The minister grew earnest. "Woman, do you realize that you have but a short time to live and that you must soon meet a holy God?"

"Yes, I realize it perfectly."

"And you are not afraid?"

"Not at all."

"And you have not made your peace with God?"

"No."

"What do you mean?" cried the astonished rector.

A smile passed over the features of the dying woman. "I have not made my peace with God because I do not need to. Christ made peace more than eighteen hundred years ago by the blood of His cross (Col. 1:20), and I am simply resting in the peace He made."

Oh, blessed is the one who has learned to rest in the peace Christ made, who counts his sins forgiven because Christ's blood was shed and God says so! ". . . We *have* our redemption through his blood, the forgiveness of our trespasses, according to the riches of his grace" (Eph. 1:7, R.V.).

3. There is a third passage very closely akin to this, that brings out the power of Christ's blood. It is I John 1:7,

*"But if we walk in the light, as he is in the light, we have
fellowship one with another, and the blood of Jesus Christ
his Son cleanseth us from all sin."*

This brings out the completeness of the forgiveness we get
through the blood. The blood of Christ has power to cleanse
the believer from *all sin*. It continually "cleanseth," is cleansing, keeping him clean every day and hour, and every minute.
The cleansing here is from the guilt of sin. When cleansing
is mentioned in the Bible in connection with the blood, it is
always cleansing from guilt. Cleansing from the power of sin
and the presence of sin is by the Word of God, the Holy Spirit,
and the living and indwelling Christ, not the crucified Christ.
Christ on the cross saves from the guilt of sin; Christ on the
throne saves from the power of sin; and Christ coming again
will save from the presence of sin. But the blood of Christ
cleanses from *all* the guilt of sin, when one is walking in the
light, submitting to the light, and walking in Christ who is
the light. The blood of Christ cleanseth him from all sin. His
past may be as bad as a past can be. There may have been
countless enormous sins, but they are all, every one, the greatest and the smallest, washed away. His record is absolutely
white in God's sight. As white as the record of Jesus Christ
Himself. His sins which were as scarlet are as white as snow,
though they were red like crimson, they are as wool (Isa.
1:18).

The blood of Christ has power to wash the blackest record
white. Some of us may have had a black past. We all have
had; for if we could see our past as God sees it before it is
washed, the record of the best of us would be black, black,
black. But if we are walking in the light, submitting to the
truth of God, believing in the light, in Christ, our record today
is white as Christ's garments were when the disciples saw Him
on the Mount of Transfiguration (Matt. 17:2, Mark 9:3,

Luke 9:29). No one can lay anything to the charge of God's elect (Rom. 8:33); there is no condemnation to them who are in Christ Jesus (Rom. 8:1).

4. Again, in Romans 5:9, we read,

> *"Much more then, being now justified by his blood, we shall be saved from wrath through him."*

The blood of Christ has power to justify. Every believer in Christ is already justified in Christ's blood. Justified means more than forgiven and cleansed. Forgiveness, as glorious as it is, is a negative thing. It means merely that our sins are put away and we are regarded as if we had not sinned. But justification is positive. It means that we are reckoned positively righteous; that positive and perfect righteousness, even the perfect righteousness of Christ, is put to our account.

It is a good thing to be stripped of vile and filthy rags, but it is far better to be clothed with garments of glory and beauty. In forgiveness we are stripped of the vile and stinking rags of our sins; in justification we are clothed upon with the glory and beauty of Christ. It is the power of the blood which secures this. In shedding His blood as a penalty for sin, Christ took our place, and when we believe in Him, we step into His place. "Him who knew no sin he made to be sin on our behalf; that we might become the righteousness of God in him" (II Cor. 5:21, R.V.).

5. Let us now look at Hebrews 9:14, R.V.,

> *"How much more shall the blood of Christ, who through the eternal Spirit offered himself without blemish unto God, cleanse your conscience from dead works to serve the living God?"*

The blood of Christ has power to cleanse the conscience from dead works to serve the living God. Do you understand what that means? It is a glorious truth and I will try to make it plain. When a man is wakened up to the fact that he is a sinner and that God is holy, he feels that he must do something to please God and atone for sin. He must "do penances," "keep Lent," or give away money, or do something else, to atone for his sins. Now all these self-efforts to please God and atone for sins are "dead works." They can never accomplish what they aim at, and can never bring peace.

How many weary years Martin Luther sought peace in this way and found it not. But when we see the power of the blood, how it has already perfectly atoned for sin, how it has already washed away our sins and justified us before God, how we are already pleasing and acceptable in God's sight *by reason of that shed blood,* then our consciences are not only relieved from the burden of guilt, but also from the burden of these self-efforts, and we are now at liberty to serve the living God, not in the slavery of fear, but in the liberty of the freedom and joy of those who know they are accepted and beloved sons. It is the blood which delivers us from the awful bondage of thinking we must do something to atone for sins and please God. The blood shows us that it is already done.

A friend of mine once said to another who was seeking peace by doing, "You have a religion of two letters. My religion is a religion of four letters."

"How is that?" asked the other.

"Your religion is *do.* My religion is *done.* You are trying to rest in what you do. I am resting in what Christ has done."

There are many Christians today who have not permitted the blood of Christ to cleanse their consciences from dead works. They are constantly feeling they must do something to atone for sin. Oh, my brother, my sister, look at what God looks at, the blood, and see that it is all *done,* already done! God is satisfied, sin is atoned for, you are justified. Now don't do dead works to commend yourself to God; but, realizing that you are already commended by the blood, serve Him in the freedom of gratitude and love, and not in the bondage of fear.

There are three classes of men. First, those who are not burdened by sin, but love it. That is wholly bad. Second, those who are burdened by sin and seek to get rid of it by self-effort. That is better, but there is something infinitely better yet. Third, those who see the hideousness of sin, and were burdened for it, but who have been brought to see the power of the blood, settling sin forever, putting it away (Heb. 9:26), and so are no longer burdened, but now work not to commend themselves to God, but out of joyous gratitude to Him who perfectly justifieth the ungodly through the shed blood.

6. In Acts 20:28, we read,

"Take heed therefore unto yourselves, and to all the flock, over the which the Holy Ghost hath made you overseers, to feed the church of God, which he hath purchased with his own blood."

And in Revelation 5:9, R.V.,

"And they sing a new song, saying, Worthy art thou to take the book, and to open the seals thereof: for thou wast slain, and didst purchase unto God with thy blood men of every tribe, and tongue, and people, and nation."

The blood of Christ has power to purchase us unto God, to make us God's own. The blood of Christ makes me God's own property. That thought brings to me a feeling of responsibility. If I belong to God, I must serve Him wholly; body, soul, and spirit, must be surrendered wholly to Him. But the thought that I am God's property brings also a feeling of security. God can and will take care of His own property. The blood of Christ has power to make me eternally secure.

7. We learn still more about the power of the blood in Hebrews 10:19, 20, R.V.,

"Having therefore, brethren, boldness to enter into the holy place by the blood of Jesus, by the way which he dedicated for us, a new and living way, through the veil, that is to say, his flesh."

The blood of Christ has power to give the believer boldness to enter into the holy place, to approach into the very presence of God. In the old Jewish days of the tabernacle and temple God manifested Himself in the most holy place. This was the place to meet God. But into this hallowed place only one Jew in all the nation was allowed to enter, the high priest; and he only once a year, on the day of atonement; and then only with blood. God was teaching the Jews, and through them the world, three great truths—God's unapproachable holiness, man's sinfulness, and that sinful man could approach a holy God only through atoning blood, that "without shedding of blood" there could be "no remission," and consequently no approach to God (Heb. 9:22). But the blood of the Old Testament sacrifices was only a figure of the true sacrifice, Jesus Christ; and, by reason of His shed blood, the vilest sinner who believes on Him has the right to approach God—come into His very presence, when he will, without fear, "in full assurance of faith," "with boldness."

Oh, the wondrous power of the blood of Christ to take all fear away when I draw near to that God who is holy and is a "consuming fire"! God is holy? Yes. And I am a sinner? Yes—but by that wondrous offering of Christ "once for all" my sin is forever put away, I am "perfected" and "justified," and, on the ground of that blood so precious and satisfying to God, I can march boldly into the very presence of God.

8. But the blood of Christ has still further power. Read Revelation 22:14, R.V.,

"Blessed are they that wash their robes, that they may have the right to come to the tree of life, and may enter in by the gates into the city."

By comparing this verse with chapter 7 and verse 14, we see that it is in the blood of Christ that robes are washed. The blood of Christ then has power to give those who believe in Him a right to the tree of life and entrance into the city of God. Sin in the first place shut men away from the tree of life and out of Eden (Gen. 3:22-24). The shed blood of Christ opens to us again the way to the tree of life and to the New Jerusalem. The blood of Christ regains for us all that Adam lost by sin, and brings us much more than was lost.

We see something of the power of the blood of Christ. Have you appreciated that blood? Have you let it have the power in your life that it ought to have? There are some today who are trying to devise a theology that leaves out the blood of Christ. Poor fools! Christianity without atoning blood is a Christianity without mercy for the sinner, without settled peace for the conscience, without genuine forgiveness, without justification, without cleansing, without boldness in approaching God, without power. It is not Christianity, but the Devil's own counterfeit. If we would know fullness of power in Christian life and service, we must first of all know the power of the blood of Christ, for it is that which brings us pardon, justification, and boldness in our approach to God. We cannot know the power of the Spirit unless we first know the power of the blood. We certainly cannot know the power of prayer unless we know the power of that blood by which alone we can approach unto God.

There are some teachers of "the higher life" who ignore the fundamental truth about the blood. They are trying to build a lofty superstructure without a firm foundation. It is bound to tumble. We must begin with the blood, if we are to go on to the "holy of holies." The brazen altar where blood was shed first met every priest who would enter into the holy place. There is no other way of entrance there. If we do not learn the lesson of this chapter, it is vain for us to try to learn the lessons of chapters 3 and 4. To everyone who wishes to know the power of the Spirit we first put the question, "Do you know the power of the blood?"

CHAPTER III

The Power of the Holy Spirit

"*POWER BELONGETH unto God.*" The Holy Spirit is the person who imparts to the individual believer the power that belongs to God. This is the Holy Spirit's work in the believer, to take what belongs to God and make it ours. All the manifold power of God belongs to the children of God as their birthright in Christ. "All things are your's" (I Cor. 3:21). But all that belongs to us as our birthright in Christ becomes ours in actual and experimental possession through the Holy Spirit's work in us as individuals. To the extent that we understand and claim for ourselves the Holy Spirit's work, to that extent do we obtain for ourselves the fullness of power in Christian life and service that God has provided for us in Christ. A very large portion of the church knows and claims for itself a very small part of that which God has made possible for them in Christ, because they know so little of what the Holy Spirit can do for us, and longs to do for us. Let us study the Word, then, to find out what the Holy Spirit has power to do in men.

We shall not go far before we discover that the same work which we see ascribed in one place to the power of the Word of God is in other places ascribed to the Holy Spirit. The explanation of this is simple. The Word of God is the instrument through which the Holy Spirit does His work. The Word of God is "the sword of the Spirit" (Eph. 6:17). The Word of God is also the seed the Spirit sows and quickens (Luke 8:11; I Pet. 1:23). The Word of God is the instrument of all the manifold operations of the Holy Spirit, as seen in Chapter I.

If, therefore, we wish the Holy Spirit to do His work in our hearts, we must study the Word. If we wish Him to do His work in the hearts of others, we must give them the Word. But the bare Word will not do the work alone. The Spirit must Himself use the Word. It is when the Spirit Himself uses His own sword that it manifests its real temper, keenness and power. God's work is accomplished by the Word and the Spirit, or rather by the Spirit through the Word. The secret of effectual living is knowing the power of the Spirit through the Word. The secret of effectual service is using the Word in the power of the Spirit. There are some who seek to magnify the Spirit but neglect the Word. This will not do at all. Fanaticism, baseless enthusiasm, wildfire are the result. Others seek to magnify the Word, but largely ignore the Spirit. Neither will this do. It leads to dead orthodoxy, truth without life and power. The true course is to recognize the instrumental power of the Word through which the Holy Spirit works, and the living, personal power of the Holy Spirit who acts through the Word.

But let us come directly to the consideration of our subject: What has the Holy Spirit power to do?

1. Turn to I Corinthians 12:3,

"Wherefore I give you to understand, that no man speaking by the Spirit of God calleth Jesus accursed: and that no man can say that Jesus is the Lord, but by the Holy Ghost."

The Holy Spirit has power to reveal Jesus Christ and His glory to man. When Jesus spoke of the Spirit's coming, He said: "But when the Comforter is come, whom I will send unto you from the Father, even the Spirit of truth, which proceedeth from the Father, he shall testify of me" (John 15:26). And it is only as He does testify of Christ that men will ever come to a true knowledge of Christ. You send men to the Word to get a knowledge of Christ; but it is only as the Holy Spirit takes the Word and illuminates it, that men ever get a real living knowledge of Christ. "No man can say that Jesus is the Lord, but by the Holy Ghost." If you wish men to get a true knowledge of Jesus Christ, such a view that they will believe on Him and be saved, you must seek for them the testimony of the Holy Spirit. Neither your testimony nor that of the Word alone, will suffice, though it is your testimony, or that of the Word, which the Spirit uses.

But unless your testimony is taken up by the Holy Spirit and He Himself testifies, they will not believe. It was not merely Peter's words about Christ that convinced the Jews at Pentecost. It was the Spirit Himself bearing witness. If you wish men to see the truth about Jesus, do not depend upon your own powers of exposition and persuasion, but cast yourself upon the Holy Ghost and seek His testimony. If you wish yourself to know Jesus with a true and living knowledge, seek the witness of the Spirit through the Word. Many a man has a correct doctrinal conception of Christ, through a study of the Word, long before he has a true personal knowledge of Christ through the testimony of the living Spirit.

2. Now let us turn to John 16:8-11:

"And when he is come, he will reprove the world of sin, and of righteousness, and of judgment: Of sin, because they believe not on me; Of righteousness, because I go to my Father, and ye see me no more; Of judgment, because the prince of this world is judged."

The Holy Spirit has power to convict the world of sin. This is closely connected with the preceding; for, it is by showing Jesus and His glory and His righteousness, that the Holy Spirit convicts of sin, and of righteousness, and of judgment. Note the sin of which the Holy Spirit convicts, "Of sin, because they believe not on me." It was so at Pentecost, as we see in Acts 2:36, 37. You can never convict any man of sin because that is the work of the Holy Spirit. You can reason and reason, and you will fail. The Holy Spirit can do it very quickly. Did you never have this experience? You have shown a man passage after passage of Scripture, and he was unmoved, and you have wondered why the man did not break down. Suddenly it has occurred to you, "Why, I am not looking in my helplessness to the mighty Spirit of God to convict this man of sin, but I am trying to convince the man of sin myself." Then you have cast yourself upon the Spirit of God for Him to do the work, and conviction came. The Spirit can convince the most careless, as experience has proven again and again.

But it is through us that the Spirit produces conviction. In John 16:7, 8, we read, ". . . I will send him unto you. And when he is come, he will reprove the world of sin, and of righteousness, and of judgment." It was the Spirit sent to Peter and the rest, who convicted the three thousand through Peter and the others on the day of Pentecost. It is ours to preach the Word and to look to the Holy Spirit to produce conviction (See Acts 2:4-37).

3. In Titus 3:5, we read,

"Not by works of righteousness which we have done, but according to his mercy he saved us, by the washing of regeneration, and renewing of the Holy Ghost."

The Holy Spirit has power to renew men or make men new, to regenerate. Regeneration is the Holy Spirit's work. He can take a man dead in trespasses and sins, and make him alive. He can take the man whose mind is blind to the truth of God, whose will is at enmity with God and set on sin, whose affections are corrupt and vile, and transform that man, impart to him God's nature, so that he thinks God's thoughts, wills what God wills, loves what God loves, and hates what God hates.

I never despair of any man when I think of the power of the Holy Spirit to make new, as I have seen it manifested again and again in the most hardened and hopeless cases. It is through us that the Holy Spirit regenerates others (I Cor. 4:15). As we have seen in Chapter I, the Word has power to regenerate; but it is not the bare word, but the word made a living thing in the heart by the power of the Holy Spirit. No amount of preaching, no matter how orthodox it is, and no amount of mere study of the Word will regenerate, unless the Holy Spirit works. Just as we are utterly dependent on the work of Christ for us in justification, so we are utterly dependent upon the work of the Holy Spirit in us in regeneration.

When one is born of the Spirit, the Spirit takes up His own abode in him (I Cor. 3:16; 6:19). The Holy Spirit dwells in everyone who belongs to Christ (Rom. 8:9). We may not have surrendered our lives very fully to this indwelling Spirit; we may be very far from being "full of the Spirit"; we may be very imperfect Christians, but, if we have been born again, the Spirit dwells in us, just as Paul said to the Corinthians, who were certainly very far from perfect Christians, that He did in them. What a glorious thought it is that the Holy Spirit dwells in me! But it is also a very solemn thought. If my body is the temple of the Holy Spirit, I certainly ought not to defile it, as many professed Christians do. Bearing in mind that our bodies are temples of the Holy Spirit would solve many problems that perplex young Christians.

4. We find a further thought about the power of the Holy Spirit in John 4:14,

"But whosoever drinketh of the water that I shall give him shall never thirst; but the water that I shall give him shall be in him a well of water springing up into everlasting life."

You may not see at first that this verse has anything to do with the Holy Spirit, but compare John 7:37, 39, and it will be evident that the water here means the Holy Spirit. The Holy Spirit, then, has power to give abiding and everlasting satisfaction. The world can never satisfy. Of every worldly joy it must be said, "Whosoever drinketh of this water shall thirst again." But the Holy Spirit has power to satisfy every longing of the soul. The Holy Spirit and He alone can satisfy the human heart. If you give yourself up to the Holy Spirit's inflowing, or rather upspringing, in your heart, you will never thirst. You will not long for the theater, or the ballroom, or the card party, or worldly gain, or honor. Oh, with what joy unutterable and satisfaction indescribable the Holy Spirit has poured forth His living water in many souls! Have you this living fountain within? Is the spring unchoked? Is it springing up into everlasting life?

5. In Romans 8:2, we read,

"For the law of the Spirit of life in Christ Jesus hath made me free from the law of sin and death."

The Holy Spirit has power to set us free from the law of sin and death. What the law of sin and death is we see in the preceding chapter (Rom. 7:9-24). Read this description carefully. We all know this law of sin and death. We have all been in bondage to it. Some of us are still in bondage to it, but we do not need to be. God has provided a way of escape. That way is by the Holy Spirit's power. When we give up the hopeless struggle of trying to overcome the law of sin and death, of trying to live right in our strength, in the power of the flesh; and in utter helplessness surrender to the Holy Spirit to do all for us; when we live after Him and walk in His blessed power; then He sets us free from the law of sin and death.

There are many professed Christians today living in Romans 7. Some go so far as to maintain that this is the normal Christian life, that one must live this life of constant defeat. This would be true, if we were left to ourselves; for in ourselves we are "carnal, sold under sin." But we are not left to ourselves. The Holy Spirit undertakes for us what we have failed to do ourselves (Rom. 8:2-4). In Romans 8 we have the picture of the true Christian life, the life that is possible to us, and that God expects from each one of us; the life where not merely the commandment comes, as in chapter 7, but where the mighty Spirit comes also, and works obedience and victory. The flesh is still in us, but we are not in the flesh (Rom. 8:12, 13, compare vs. 9). We do not live after it. We "live after the Spirit." We, "through the Spirit do mortify the deeds of the body." We "walk in the Spirit," and do "not fulfill the lust of the flesh" (Gal. 5:16). It is our privilege, in the Spirit's power, to get daily, hourly, and constant victory over the flesh and over sin. But the victory is not in ourselves, not in any strength of our own. Left to ourselves, deserted of the Spirit of God, we would be as helpless as ever. It is all in the Spirit's power. If we try to take one step in our own strength, we shall fail.

Has the Holy Spirit set you free from the law of sin and death? Will you let Him do it now? Simply give up all self-effort to be free from "the law of sin and death," to give up sinning; believe in the divine power of the Holy Spirit to set you free; and cast yourself upon Him to do it. He will do it. Then you can triumphantly cry with Paul, "For the law of the Spirit of life in Christ Jesus made me free from the law of sin and of death" (Rom. 8:2, R.V.).

6. We find a closely allied but larger thought about the Holy Spirit's power in Ephesians 3:16, R.V.,

"That he would grant you, according to the riches of his glory, that ye may be strengthened with power through his Spirit in the inward man."

The Holy Spirit strengthens the believer with power in the inward man. The result of this strengthening is seen in verses 17 to 19. Here the power of the Spirit manifests itself not merely in giving us victory over sin, but (a) in Christ's dwelling in our hearts; (b) our being "rooted and grounded in love"; (c) our being made "strong to apprehend with all the saints what is the breadth and length and height and depth, and to know the love of Christ which passeth knowledge . . ." (Eph. 3:18, 19). It all ultimates in our being "filled unto all the fulness of God."

7. We find a still further thought about the Holy Spirit's power in Romans 8:14, R.V.,

"For as many as are led by the Spirit of God, these are sons of God."

The Holy Spirit has power to lead us into a holy life, a life as "sons of God," a godlike life. Not merely does the Holy Spirit give us power to live a holy life, a life well-pleasing to God when we have discovered what that life is: He takes us by the hand, as it were, and leads us into that life. Our whole part is simply to surrender ourselves utterly to Him to lead and to mould us. Those who do this are not merely God's offspring, which all men are (Acts 17:28); neither are we merely God's children: "These are sons of God."

8. Further down in the chapter there is a new thought. Romans 8:16, R.V.,

"The Spirit himself beareth witness with our spirit, that we are children of God."

The Holy Spirit bears witness with the spirit of the believer that he is a child of God. Note that Paul does not say that the Spirit bears witness to our spirit, but with it—"together with our spirit," is the exact force of the words used. That is, there are two who bear witness to our sonship: First, our spirit bears witness that we are children of God; second, the Holy Spirit bears witness together with our spirit that we are children of God.

How does the Holy Spirit bear His testimony to this fact? Galatians 4:6 answers this question, "And because ye are sons, God sent forth the Spirit of his Son into our hearts, crying, Abba, Father" (R.V.). The Holy Spirit Himself enters into our hearts and cries, "Abba, Father." Note the order of the Spirit's work in Romans 8:2, 4, 13, 14, 16. It is only when "the law of the Spirit of life in Christ Jesus hath made me free from the law of sin and death" (v. 2), and so "the righteousness of the law might be fulfilled" in me "who walk not after the flesh, but after the Spirit" (v. 4), and I "through the Spirit of God do mortify the deeds of the body" (v. 13), and when I am surrendered to the Spirit's leading (v. 14), it is then, and only then, that I can expect verse 16 to be realized in my experience, and that I have the clear assurance of sonship that comes from the Spirit of God testifying together with my spirit, that I am a child of God. There are many seeking this testimony of the Holy Spirit in the wrong place; namely, as a condition of their surrendering wholly to God, and confessing the crucified and risen Lord as their Saviour and Lord. The testimony of the Holy Spirit to our sonship comes after all this is done.

9. An exceedingly important thought about the Holy Spirit's power is found in Galatians 5:22, 23,

> *"But the fruit of the Spirit is love, joy, peace, longsuffering, gentleness, goodness, faith, Meekness, temperance: against such there is no law."*

The Holy Spirit brings forth in the believer Christlike graces of character (Compare Rom. 5:5; 14:17; 15:13). All real beauty of character, all real Christlikeness in us, is the Holy Spirit's work. It is His "fruit." He bears it; not we. Note that these graces are not said to be the fruits of the Spirit; they are the "fruit." There is a unity of origin running all through the multiplicity of manifestation; and not some of these graces, but all, will appear in everyone in whom the Holy Spirit is given full control.

It is a beautiful life that is set forth in these verses. Every word is worthy of earnest study and profound meditation: "Love," "joy," "peace," "longsuffering," "gentleness," "goodness," "faith," "meekness," "self-control." Is not this the life we all long for, the Christ life? It is not natural to us, and it is not attainable by any effort of "the flesh," or nature. The life that is natural for us is set forth in the three preceding verses (19-21). But when the indwelling Spirit is given full control in the one He inhabits; when we are brought to realize the utter badness of the flesh, and give up in helpless despair of ever attaining to anything really good in its power; when, in other words, we come to the end of self, and just give over the whole work of making us what we ought to be to the indwelling HOLY SPIRIT, then, and only then, these holy graces of character are His "fruit."

Do you wish these graces in your character and life? Renounce self utterly, and all its strivings after holiness; and let the Holy Spirit, who dwells in you, take full control and bear His own glorious fruit. We get the same essential truth from another point of view in Galatians 2:20 (R.V., Am. App.), "I have been crucified with Christ; and it is no longer I that live, but Christ liveth in me: and that life which I now live in the flesh I live in faith, the faith which is in the Son of God, who loved me, and gave himself up for me."

Settle it clearly and forever that the flesh can never bear

this fruit, that you can never attain these things by your own effort, that they are "the fruit of the Spirit." We hear a good deal in these days about "ethical culture," which usually means a cultivation of the flesh until it bears the fruit of the Spirit. It cannot be done, until thorns can be made to bear figs, and a bramblebush, grapes (Matt. 12:33; Luke 6:44). We hear also a good deal about "character building." That is all very well, if you let the Holy Spirit do the building, and then it is not so much building as fruit-bearing. (See, however, II Pet. 1:5-7.) We hear also about "cultivating graces of character," but we must always bear in mind that the way to cultivate true graces of character is by submitting ourselves utterly to the Spirit to do His work. This is "sanctification of the Spirit" (I Pet. 1:2; II Thess. 2:13).

We turn now to the power of the Holy Spirit in a different direction.

10. John 16:13, R.V.:

> "Howbeit when he, the Spirit of truth, is come, he shall guide you into all the truth: for he shall not speak from himself; but what things soever he shall hear, these shall he speak: and he shall declare unto you the things that are to come."

The Holy Spirit has power to guide the believer "into all the truth." This promise was made in the first instance to the apostles, but the apostles themselves applied it to all believers (I John 2:20, 27). It is the privilege of each of us to be "taught of God." Each believer is independent of human teachers. "Ye need not that any man teach you." This does not mean, of course, that we may not learn much from others, who are taught by the Holy Spirit. If John had thought that, he would never have written this epistle to teach others. The man who is most fully taught of God is the very one who will be most ready to listen to what God has taught others. Much less does it mean that when we are taught of God we are independent of the Word of God. For the Word is the very place to which the Spirit leads His pupils, and the instrument through which He teaches them (John 6:63; Eph. 6:17; Eph. 5:18, 19; Comp. Col. 3:16). But, while we may learn much from men, we are not dependent upon them. We have a divine teacher, the Holy Spirit.

We shall never truly know the truth until we are thus taught. No amount of mere human teaching, no matter who our teachers may be, will give us a correct apprehension of the truth. Not even a diligent study of the Word, either in the English or original languages, will give us a real understanding of the truth. We must be taught of the Holy Spirit. And we may be thus taught, each one of us. The one who is thus taught, even if he does not know a word of Greek or Hebrew, will understand the truth of God better than the one who knows the Greek, and Hebrew, and all "the cognate languages," and is not taught of the Spirit. The Spirit will guide the one He teaches "into all the truth," not in a day, or in a week, or in a year, but step by step.

There are two especial lines of the Spirit's teaching mentioned. (a) "He shall declare unto you the things that are to come." Many say we can know nothing of the future, that all our thoughts on that subject are guesswork. Anyone taught of the Spirit knows better than that. (b) "He shall glorify me [i.e., Christ]: for he shall take of mine, and shall declare it unto you." This is the Holy Spirit's especial line, with the believer as well as the unbeliever, to declare unto them the things of Christ and glorify Him.

Many fear to emphasize the truth about the Holy Spirit, lest Christ be disparaged. But no one magnifies Christ as the Holy Spirit does. We will never understand Christ, nor see His glory, until the Holy Spirit interprets Him to us. The mere listening to sermons and lectures, the mere study of the Word even,

will never give you to see the things of Christ. The Holy Spirit
must show you, and He is willing to do it. He is longing to
do it. I suppose the Holy Spirit's inmost desire is to reveal
Jesus Christ to men. Let Him do it. Christ is so different when
the Holy Spirit glorifies Him by taking of the things of Christ
and showing them unto us.

11. Turning to John 14:26, R.V., we find again the Holy
Spirit's power to teach, but with an added thought,

> "But the Comforter, even the Holy Spirit, whom the
> Father will send in my name, he shall teach you all things,
> and bring to your remembrance all that I said unto you."

The Holy Spirit has power to bring to remembrance the
words of Christ. This promise was made primarily to the
apostles, and is the guarantee of the accuracy of their report
of what Jesus said. But the Holy Spirit does a similar work
with each believer who expects it of Him and looks to Him
to do it. He brings to mind the teachings of Christ, and the
words of Christ, just when we need them, for either the neces-
sities of our own life or of our service.

How many of us could tell of occasions when we were in
great distress of soul, of great questioning concerning our duty,
or great extremity as to what to say to one whom we were trying to lead to Christ, or to help; and just the Scripture we
needed, some passage we had not thought of for a long time,
and, perhaps, never thought of in this connection, was brought
to mind. It was the Holy Spirit who did this, and He is ready
to do it even more, when we expect it of Him.

Is it without significance, that in the next verse after making
this great promise, Jesus says: "Peace I leave with you; my
peace I give unto you"? Look to the Holy Spirit to bring the
right words to remembrance at the right time, and you will
have peace. This is the way to remember Scripture, just when
you need it, and just the Scripture you need.

12. Closely akin to what has been said in the two preceding sections is the power of the Holy Spirit as seen in I Corinthians 2:10-14, R.V.:

> "But unto us God revealed them through the Spirit: for the Spirit searcheth all things, yea, the deep things of God. For who among men knoweth the things of a man, save the spirit of the man, which is in him? even so the things of God none knoweth, save the Spirit of God. But we received, not the spirit of the world, but the spirit which is from God; that we might know the things that were freely given to us of God. Which things also we speak, not in words which man's wisdom teacheth, but which the Spirit teacheth; combining spiritual things with spiritual words. Now the natural man receiveth not the things of the Spirit of God: for they are foolishness unto him; and he cannot know them, because they are spiritually judged."

In these verses we have a twofold work of the Spirit: (a) The Holy Spirit reveals to us the deep things of God, which are hidden from and foolishness to the natural man. It is preeminently to the apostles that He does this, but we cannot limit this work of the Spirit to them. (b) The Holy Spirit interprets His own revelation, or imparts power to discern, know, and appreciate what He has taught.

Not only is the Holy Spirit the author of Revelation—the written Word of God. He is also the interpreter of what He has revealed. How much more interesting and helpful any deep book becomes when we have the author of the book right at hand to interpret it to us! This is what we always may have when we study the Bible. The author—the Holy Spirit—is right at hand to interpret. To understand the book we must look to Him. Then the darkest places become clear. We need to pray often with the psalmist, "Open thou mine eyes, that I may behold wondrous things out of thy law" (Psa. 119:18).

It is not enough that we have the objective revelation in the written word; we must also have the inward illumination of the Holy Spirit to enable us to comprehend it. It is a great mistake to try to comprehend a spiritual revelation with the natural understanding. It is the foolish attempt to do this that has landed so many in the bog of the higher criticism. A man with no aesthetic sense might as well expect to appreciate the Sistine Madonna, because he is not color blind, as an unspiritual man to understand the Bible, simply because he understands the laws of grammar and the vocabulary of the language in which the Bible was written. I would as soon think of setting a man to teach art merely because he understood paints, as to set him to teach the Bible merely because he understood Greek or Hebrew.

We all need not only to recognize the utter insufficiency and worthlessness of our own righteousness, which is the lesson of the opening chapters of the epistle to the Romans, but also the utter insufficiency and worthlessness in the things of God, of our own wisdom, which is the lesson of the first epistle to the Corinthians, especially the first to the third chapters (see *e.g.* I Cor. 1:19-21, 26, 27).

The Jews had a revelation by the Spirit but they failed to depend upon Him to interpret it to them, so they went astray. The whole evangelical church realizes the utter insufficiency of man's righteousness, theoretically at least. Now it needs to be taught, and made to feel, the utter insufficiency of man's wisdom. That is perhaps the lesson this nineteenth century of overweening intellectual conceit needs most of any.

To understand God's Word, we must empty ourselves utterly of our own wisdom and rest in utter dependence upon the Spirit of God to interpret it to us (Matt. 11:25). When we put away our own righteousness, then, and only then, we get the righteousness of God (Phil. 3:4-7, 9; Rom. 10:3). When we put away our own wisdom, then, and only then, we get the wisdom of God (Matt. 11:25; I Cor. 3:18; I Cor. 1:25-28). When we put away our own strength, then, and only then, we get the strength of God (Isa. 40:29; II Cor. 12:9; I Cor. 1:27, 28). Emptying must precede filling—self poured out that Christ may be poured in. We must be daily taught of the Spirit to understand the Word.

I cannot depend today on the fact that the Spirit taught me yesterday. Each new contact with the Word must be in the power of the Spirit. That the Holy Spirit once illumined our mind to grasp a certain passage is not enough. He must do so each time we confront that passage.

Andrew Murray has put this truth well. He says, "Each time you come to the Word in study, in hearing a sermon or reading a religious book, there ought to be as distinct as your intercourse with the external means, a definite act of self-abnegation, denying your own wisdom and yielding yourself in faith to the divine teacher" (*The Spirit of Christ*, p. 221).

13. The Holy Spirit has not only power to teach us the truth, but also to impart power to us in communicating that truth to others. We see this brought out again and again.

"And I, brethren, when I came unto you, came not with excellency of speech or of wisdom, proclaiming to you the testimony of God. For I determined not to know anything among you, save Jesus Christ, and him crucified. And I was with you in weakness, and in fear, and in much trembling. And my speech and my preaching were not in persuasive words of wisdom, but in demonstration of the Spirit and of power: that your faith should not stand in the wisdom of men, but in the power of God."—I Cor. 2:1-5, R.V.

"Our gospel came not unto you in word only, but also in power, and in the Holy Ghost" (I Thess. 1:5). "But ye shall

receive power, after that the Holy Ghost is come upon you"
(Acts 1:8). The Holy Spirit enables the believer to communicate to others in "power" the truth he himself has been taught.
We not only need the Holy Spirit to reveal the truth in the
first place; and the Holy Spirit in the second place to interpret
to us as individuals the truth He has revealed; but in the third
place we also need the Holy Spirit to enable us to effectually
communicate to others the truth He Himself has interpreted
to us. We need Him all along the line. One great cause of
real failure in the ministry, even when there is seeming success,
and not only in the ministry but in all forms of service by
Christian men and women, is from the attempt to teach by
"enticing words of man's wisdom," *i.e.,* by the arts of human
logic, rhetoric or eloquence, what the Holy Spirit has taught
us. What is needed is Holy Ghost power, "demonstration of
the Spirit and of power."

There are three causes of failure in Christian work. First,
some other message is taught than the message which the Holy
Spirit has revealed in the Word. Men preach science, art,
philosophy, sociology, history, experience, etc., etc., and not
the simple Word of God as found in the Holy Spirit's Book—
the Bible. Second, the Spirit-taught message, the Bible, is
studied and sought to be comprehended by the natural understanding, *i.e.,* without the Spirit's illumination. Third, the
Spirit-given message, the Word, the Bible, studied and comprehended under the Holy Spirit's illumination, is given out to
others with "enticing words of man's wisdom," and not "in
demonstration of the Spirit and of power." We need, we are
absolutely dependent upon, the Holy Spirit all along the line.
He must teach us how to speak as well as what to speak. He
must be the power as well as the message.

14. The Holy Spirit has power to teach us how to pray. In
Jude 20, R.V., we read,

"But ye, beloved, building up yourselves on your most holy faith, praying in the Holy Spirit."

Again in Ephesians, 6:18, R.V.,

"Praying at all seasons in the Spirit."

The Holy Spirit guides the believer in prayer. The disciples did not know how to pray as they ought, so they came to Jesus and said: "Lord, teach us to pray" (Luke 11:1). "We know not how to pray as we ought," but we have another helper right at hand to help us (John 14:16, 17). "The Spirit also helpeth our infirmity" (Rom. 8:26, R.V.). He teacheth us to pray. True prayer is prayer "in the Spirit," *i.e.,* the prayer which the Spirit inspires and directs. When we come into God's presence to pray, we should recognize our infirmity, our ignorance of what we should pray for or how we should pray, and, in the consciousness of our utter inability to pray aright, look up to the Holy Spirit and cast ourselves utterly upon Him to direct our prayers, to lead out our desires, and guide our utterance of them. Rushing heedlessly into God's presence, and asking the first thing that comes into our minds, or that some thoughtless one asks us to pray for, is not "praying in the Holy Ghost," and is not true prayer. We must wait for the Holy Spirit, and surrender ourselves to the Holy Spirit. The prayer that God the Holy Spirit inspires is the prayer that God the Father answers. From Romans 8:26, 27, we learn that the longings which the Holy Spirit begets in our hearts are often too deep for utterance; too deep, apparently, for clear and definite comprehension on the part of the believer himself, in whom the Holy Spirit is working. God Himself must "search the heart," to know "what is the mind of the Spirit" in these unuttered and unutterable longings. But God does know "what is the mind of the Spirit." He does know what those Spirit-given longings mean, even if we do not, and these longings are "according to the will of God," and He grants them. So it comes that He is "able to do exceeding abundantly above all that we ask or think, according to the power that worketh in us" (Eph. 3:20). There are other times when the Spirit's leadings in prayer are so plain that we 'pray with the Spirit and with the understanding also' (I Cor. 14:15).

15. The Holy Spirit has also power to lead out our hearts in acceptable thanksgiving to God. Paul says:

". . . Be filled with the Spirit; speaking one to another in psalms and hymns and spiritual songs, singing and making melody with your heart to the Lord; giving thanks always for all things in the name of our Lord Jesus Christ to God, even the Father."—Eph. 5:18-20, R.V.

Not only does the Spirit teach us to pray, He also teaches us to render thanks. One of the most prominent characteristics of the "Spirit-filled life" is thanksgiving. True thanksgiving is "to God, even the Father," "in the name of our Lord Jesus Christ," "in the Holy Spirit."

16. The Holy Spirit has power to inspire in the heart of the believer in Christ worship that is acceptable to God.

"For we are the circumcision, who worship by the Spirit of God, and glory in Christ Jesus, and have no confidence in the flesh."—Phil. 3:3, R.V.

Prayer is not worship, thanksgiving is not worship. Worship is a definite act of the creature in relation to God. Worship is bowing before God in adoring acknowledgment and contemplation of Himself. Someone has said, "In our prayers we are taken up with our needs; in our thanksgivings we are taken up with our blessings; in our worship we are taken up with Himself." There is no true and acceptable worship except that which the Holy Spirit prompts and directs. "Such doth the Father seek to be his worshippers" (John 4:23, R.V.).

The flesh seeks to enter every sphere of life. It has its worship as well as its lust. The worship which the flesh prompts is an abomination to God. Not all earnest and honest worship is worship in the Spirit. A man may be very honest and very earnest in his worship, and still not have submitted himself to the guidance of the Holy Spirit in the matter, and so his worship is in the flesh. Even where there is great loyalty to the letter of the Word, worship may not be "in the Spirit," *i.e.,* inspired and directed by Him. To worship aright we must "have no confidence in the flesh." We must recognize the utter inability of the flesh, *i.e.,* our natural self as contrasted with the divine Spirit who dwells in and should mould everything in the believer, to worship acceptably. We must realize also the danger there is that the flesh, self, intrude itself into our worship. In utter self-distrust and self-abnegation we must cast ourselves upon the Holy Spirit, to lead us aright in our worship. Just as we must renounce any merit in ourselves, and cast ourselves utterly upon Christ and His work for us for justification; just so we must renounce any capacity for good in ourselves, and cast ourselves utterly upon the Holy Spirit, and His work in us, in living, praying, thanking, and worshipping, and all else that we are to do.

17. Let us next consider the Holy Spirit's power as a guide. In Acts 13:2-4, we read:

> *"As they ministered to the Lord, and fasted, the Holy Ghost said, Separate me Barnabas and Saul for the work whereunto I have called them. And when they had fasted and prayed, and laid their hands on them, they sent them away. So they, being sent forth by the Holy Ghost, departed unto Seleucia; and from thence they sailed to Cyprus."*

The Holy Spirit calls men and sends them forth to definite lines of work. The Holy Spirit not only calls men in a general way into Christian work, but He also selects the specific work and points it out. "Shall I go to China, to Africa, to India?" many a one is asking, and many another ought to ask. You cannot rightly settle that question for yourselves, neither can any other man settle it rightly for you. Not every Christian man is called to China or Africa or any other foreign field. God alone knows whether He wishes you to go to any of these places. He is willing to show you.

How does the Holy Spirit call? The passage before us does not tell. It is presumably purposely silent on this point, lest, perhaps, we think that He must always call in precisely the same way. There is nothing to indicate that He spoke by an audible voice, much less that He made his will known in any of the fantastic ways in which some profess to discern His leading, as, e.g., by some twitching of the body, or by opening the Bible at random, and putting the finger on a passage that may be construed into some entirely different meaning than that which the inspired writer intended by it. But the important point is that He made His will clearly known. He is as willing to make His will clearly known to us today. The great need in Christian work today is men and women whom the Holy Spirit calls and sends forth. We have plenty of men and women whom men have called and sent forth; we have far too many who have called themselves. There are many today who object strenuously to being sent forth by men, by any organization of any kind, who are, what is immeasurably worse than that, sent forth by themselves, not by God. How shall we receive the Holy Spirit's call? By desiring it, seeking it, waiting upon the Lord for it, and expecting it. "As they ministered to the Lord, and fasted," the record reads.

Many a man is saying, in self-justification for staying out of the ministry, or for staying home from the foreign field: "I have never had a call." How do you know that? Have you been listening for it? God speaks often in a still small voice.

Only the listening ear can catch it. Have you definitely offered yourself to God to send you where He will? While no man ought to go to China or Africa unless he is clearly and definitely called, he ought to definitely offer himself to God for this work, and be ready for a call, and listening sharply that he may hear it when it comes. No educated Christian man or woman has a right to rest easy out of the foreign field until they have definitely offered themselves to God for that work, and it is clear no call from God has come. Indeed, a man needs no more definite call to Africa than to Boston, or New York, or Chicago.

18. We learn something further about the Holy Spirit's power to guide in Acts 8:27-29. First, we have the story of Philip:

> *"And he arose and went: and, behold, a man of Ethiopia, an eunuch of great authority under Candace queen of the Ethiopians, who had the charge of all her treasure, and had come to Jerusalem for to worship, Was returning, and sitting in his chariot read Esaias the prophet. Then the Spirit said unto Philip, Go near, and join thyself to this chariot."*

Second, the second word is about Paul and his missionary party:

> *"And they went through the region of Phrygia and Galatia, having been forbidden of the Holy Spirit to speak the word in Asia; and when they were come over against Mysia, they assayed to go into Bithynia; and the Spirit of Jesus suffered them not."*—Acts 16:6, 7, R.V.

The Holy Spirit guides in the details of daily life and service as to where to go and where not to go, what to do and what not to do. It is possible for us to have the unerring guidance of the Holy Spirit at every turn in our lives. For example, in personal work it is manifestly not God's intention that

we speak to everyone we meet. There are some to whom we
ought not to speak. Time spent on them would be time taken
from work which would be more to the glory of God. Doubtless Philip met many as he journeyed toward Gaza, before he
met the one of whom the Spirit said: "Go near, and join thyself to this chariot." In the same way is He ready to guide us
in our personal work. He is ready also to guide us in all the
affairs of life: business, study, social life—everything. We can
have God's wisdom, if we will, at every turn of life. There
is no promise more plain and explicit than James 1:5: "If
any of you lack wisdom, let him ask of God, that giveth to
all men liberally, and upbraideth not; and it shall be given
him." How shall we gain this wisdom? James 1:5-7 answers.
Here are really five steps.

First: That we "lack wisdom." We must be conscious of
and fully admit our own inability to decide wisely. Not only
the sinfulness but the wisdom of the flesh must be renounced.

Second: We must really desire to know God's way, and be
willing to do God's will. This is implied in the asking, if the
asking be sincere. This is a point of fundamental importance.
Here we find the reason why men ofttimes do not know God's
will, and have not the Spirit's guidance. They are not really
willing to do whatever the Spirit leads. It is "the meek" whom
He guides in judgment, and the meek to whom "he will teach
his way" (Psa. 25:9). It is he who "willeth to do his will"
who "shall know" (John 7:17, R.V.).

Third: We must ask, definitely ask guidance.

Fourth: We must confidently expect guidance.

"Let him ask in faith, nothing doubting" (vss. 6 and 7,
R.V.).

Fifth: We must follow step by step as the guidance comes.
Just how it will come no one can tell. But it will come. It
may come with only a step made clear at a time. That is all
that we need to know—the next step. Many are in darkness

because they do not know what God will have them to do next week, or next month, or next year. Do you know the next step? That is enough. Take it, and then He will show you the next. (See Num. 9:17-23.) God's guidance is clear guidance (I John 1:5). Many are tortured by leadings which they fear may be from God, but which they are not sure about. You have a right, as God's child, to be sure. Go to God and say: "Here I am, heavenly Father; I am willing to do Thy will, but make it clear. If this is Thy will, I will do it; but make it clear if it is." He will do it, if it is His will and you are willing to do it. You need not and ought not to do that thing until He does make it clear. We have no right to dictate to God how He shall give His guidance, as, *e.g.,* by "shutting up every other way," or by a sign, or by letting us put our finger on a text. It is ours to seek and expect wisdom, but it is not ours to dictate how it shall be given (I Cor. 12:11).

19. In one more direction has the Holy Spirit power. Read Acts 4:31; 13:9, 10,

> *"And when they had prayed, the place was shaken where they were assembled together; and they were all filled with the Holy Ghost, and they spake the word of God with boldness."*

The Holy Spirit has power to give us boldness in testimony for Christ. Many are naturally timid. They long to do something for Christ, but they are afraid. The Holy Spirit can make you bold if you will look to Him and trust Him to do it. It was He who turned the craven Peter into the one who fearlessly faced the Sanhedrin and rebuked their sin. (See Acts 4:8-12.)

Two things are manifest from what has been said about the power of the Holy Spirit in the believer: First, how utterly dependent we are upon the Holy Spirit at every turn of Christian life and service. Second, how perfect is the provision for life and service that God has made, and what the fullness of privilege that is open to the humblest believer, through the Holy Spirit's work. It is not so much what we are by nature either intellectually, morally, spiritually, or even physically that is important; but what the Holy Spirit can do for us, and what we will let Him do. The Holy Spirit often takes the one who gives the least natural promise and uses him far more than those who give the greatest natural promise. Christian life is not to be lived in the realm of natural temperament, and Christian work is not to be done in the power of natural endowment but Christian life is to be lived in the realm of the Spirit, and Christian work is to be done in the power of the Holy Ghost. The Holy Spirit is eagerly desirous to do for each of us His whole work. He will do for each of us all we will let Him do.

CHAPTER IV

The Power of Prayer

"*POWER BELONGETH unto God,*" but all that belongs to God we can have for the asking. God holds out His full hands and says: "Ask, and it shall be given you. . . . If ye then, being evil, know how to give good gifts unto your children, how much more shall your Father which is in heaven give good things to them that ask him?" (Matt. 7:7, 11). The poverty and powerlessness of the average Christian finds its explanation in the words of the Apostle James: "Ye have not, because ye ask not" (Jas. 4:2).

"Why is it," many a Christian is asking, "that I make such poor progress in my Christian life?"

"Neglect of prayer," God answers. "You have not because you ask not."

"Why is it there is so little fruit in my ministry?" asks many a discouraged minister.

"Neglect of prayer," God answers again. "You have not because you ask not."

"Why is it," many, both ministers and laymen, are asking, "that there is so little power in my life and service?"

And again God answers: "Neglect of prayer. You have not because you ask not."

God has provided for a life of power, and a work of power on the part of every child of His. He has put His own infinite power at our disposal, and has proclaimed over and over again, in a great variety of ways in His Word, "Ask, and ye shall receive." Thousands upon thousands have taken God at His word in this matter, and have always found it true. The first Christians were men of tremendous power. What power Peter and John, for example, had in their lives! What power they had in their work! There was opposition in those days—most determined, bitter, and relentless opposition; opposition in comparison with which that which we encounter is but as child's play—but the work went right on.

We constantly read such statements as these: "And the Lord added to the church daily such as should be saved" (Acts 2:47). "Howbeit many of them which heard the word believed; and the number of the men was about five thousand" (Acts 4:4). "And believers were the more added to the Lord, multitudes both of men and women" (Acts 5:14). The apostles themselves explain the secret of their resistless power when they say: "But we will give ourselves continually to prayer, and to the ministry of the word" (Acts 6:4).

But it was not only the leaders who had power in life and service; so had the rank and file of that early church. What a beautiful picture we have of the abounding love and fruitfulness of that early church! (Acts 2:44-47; 4:32-37; 8:4; 11:19, 21). The secret of this fullness of power in life and service is found in Acts 2:42, "They continued stedfastly . . . in prayers." God delights to answer prayer. "Call upon me . . . ," He cries, "I will deliver thee, and thou shalt glorify me" (Psa. 50:15). There is a place where strength can always be renewed; that place is the presence of the Lord. "But they that wait upon the Lord shall renew their strength; they shall mount up with wings as eagles; they shall run, and not be weary; and they shall walk, and not faint" (Isa. 40:31).

How little time the average Christian spends in prayer! We are too busy to pray, and so we are too busy to have power. We have a great deal of activity but we accomplish little; many services but few conversions; much machinery but few results. The power of God is lacking in our lives and in our work. We have not because we ask not. Many professed Christians confessedly do not believe in the power of prayer. It is quite the fashion with some to contemptuously contrast the pray-ers with the do-ers—forgetting that in the history of the church the real do-ers have been pray-ers, that the men who have made the glorious part of the church's history have been, without exception, men of prayer. Of those who do believe theoretically in the power of prayer, not one in a thousand realizes its power.

How much time does the average Christian spend daily in prayer? How much time do you spend daily in prayer? It was a master stroke of the Devil when he got the church and the ministry so generally to lay aside the mighty weapon of prayer. The Devil is perfectly willing that the church should multiply its organizations and its deftly-contrived machinery for the conquest of the world for Christ, if it will only give up praying. He laughs softly, as he looks at the church of today, and says under his breath: "You can have your Sunday Schools, and your Y.M.C.A.'s, and your Y.W.C.A.'s, and your Y.P.S.C.E.'s, and your B.Y.P.U.'s, and your Epworth Leagues, and your W.C.T.U.'s, and your Boys' Brigades, and your Institutional Churches, and your Men's Clubs, and your grand choirs, and your fine organs, and your brilliant preachers, and your revival efforts, even, if you do not bring into them the power of Almighty God, sought and obtained by earnest, persistent, believing, mighty prayer." The Devil is not afraid of machinery; he is only afraid of God, and machinery without prayer is machinery without God.

Our day is characterized by the multiplication of man's machinery and the diminution of God's power sought and obtained by prayer. But when men and women arise who believe in prayer, and who pray in the way the Bible teaches us to pray, prayer accomplishes as much as it ever did. Prayer can do today as much as it ever could. Prayer can do anything God can do; for the arm of God responds to the touch of prayer. All the infinite resources of God are at the command of prayer. Prayer is the key that opens wide the inexhaustible storehouses of divine grace and power. "Ask, and it shall be given you," cries our heavenly Father as He swings wide open the doors of the divine treasure house. There is only one limit to what prayer can do; that is what God can do. But all things are possible to God; therefore prayer is omnipotent.

Christian history and Christian biography demonstrate the truth of what the Word of God teaches about prayer. All through the history of the Church, men and women have arisen in all ranks of life who believed with simple, childlike faith what the Bible teaches about prayer, and they have asked and they have received . But what are some of the definite things that prayer has power to do?

1. Prayer has power to bring a true knowledge of ourselves and our needs. There is nothing more necessary than that we know ourselves, our weakness, our sinfulness, our selfishness; how that in us, that is to say in our flesh, dwelleth no good thing (Rom. 7:18). Lives of power have usually begun with a revelation of the utter powerlessness and worthlessness of self. So it was with Isaiah. In the year that king Uzziah died, he was brought face to face with God, and saw himself, and cried out: "Woe is me! for I am undone; because I am a man of unclean lips" (Isa. 6:5). Then a life of power began for Isaiah and God sent him forth to a mighty work (Isa. 6:8, 9). It was so with Moses. He met God at the burning bush, and was emptied of his former self-confidence, saw his utter unfitness for the Lord's work, and then the Lord sent him as a mighty man of power (Exod. 3:2, 5, 11. Comp. Exod. 2:11-15). It was so with Job. It was after Job met God, and cried concerning himself: "I abhor myself, and repent in dust and ashes," that the Lord turned the captivity of Job, and that he

received power to intercede for his friends, and to bear abundant fruit (Job 42:5, 6, 10, 12).

It is needful, if we are to have fullness of power, that we get a view of ourselves as we are by nature. It is in prayer that we get it. If we sincerely pray the psalmist's prayer: "Search me, O God, and know my heart: try me, and know my thoughts" (Psa. 139:23), He will do it. There will come a true revelation of self as God sees us, a consequent utter emptying of self, and room will be made for the incoming of the power of God. It is not enough to pray this prayer once for all. It needs to be repeated daily.

2. Prayer has power to cleanse our hearts from sin; from secret sin and from known sin (Psa. 19:12, 13). In answer to David's prayer after his disastrous fall, God washed him thoroughly from his iniquity, and cleansed him from his sin (Psa. 51:2). Many a man has fought for days and months and years against some sin that has been marring his life and sapping his spiritual power, and at last has gone unto God in prayer, and held on to God, and would not let Him go until He blessed him; and he has come out of the place of prayer a victor. In this way sins that seem unconquerable have been laid in the dust. In this way the secret sin that the sinner himself scarce discerned, but that has robbed him of power, has been discovered in all its real hideousness, and rooted out. Of course, as seen in the previous chapter, it is the Holy Spirit who sets us free from sin's power, but the Holy Spirit works in our lives in answer to our prayers (Luke 11:13).

3. Prayer has power to hold us up in our goings, and give us victory over temptation. "Hold up my goings in thy paths, that my footsteps slip not," cried David (Psa. 17:5). That is a prayer God is ever ready to hear. Jesus Himself said to His disciples, as the hour of trial drew nigh, "Pray that ye enter not into temptation" (Luke 22:40). But the disciples did not heed the warning. They slept when they should have prayed,

and when the temptation came in a few hours, they failed utterly. But Jesus Himself spent that night in prayer, and the next day when the fiercest temptations that ever beset a son of man swept down upon Him, He came off gloriously triumphant. We can come off victorious over every temptation if we will prepare for it and meet it by prayer. Many of us are led into defeat and denial of our Lord, as Peter was, by sleeping when we ought to be praying.

4. Prayer has power to govern our tongues. Many a Christian who has desired fullness of power in Christian life and service, has found himself kept from it by an unruly tongue. He has learned by bitter experience the truth of the words of James: "The tongue can no man tame" (Jas. 3:8). But while no man can tame it, God can and will, in answer to believing prayer. If one will earnestly and believingly pray with David: "Set a watch, O Lord, before my mouth; keep the door of my lips" (Psa. 141:3), God will do it. Many and many an unruly tongue has been brought into subjection in this way. Tongues that were as sharp as the piercings of a sword, have learned to speak words of gentleness and grace. True prayer can tame the unruliest tongue by which man or woman was ever cursed, because true prayer brings into play the power of Him with whom nothing is impossible.

5. Prayer has power to bring us wisdom. The Word of God is very explicit on this point: "If any of you lack wisdom, let him ask of God, that giveth to all men liberally, and upbraideth not; and it shall be given him" (Jas. 1:5). No promise could be more explicit than that. We can have wisdom, the wisdom of God Himself, at every turn of life. God does not intend that His children shall grope in darkness. He puts His own infinite wisdom at our disposal. All He asks is that we ask, and ask in faith (Jas. 1:6-7). Many of us are stumbling on in our own foolishness, instead of walking on in His wisdom, simply because we do not ask. He greatly desires us to

know His way, and is willing to make it known upon our asking. Oh, the joy of knowing and walking in God's way! And we can all have this joy for the asking (Psa. 86:11; 25:4; 143:10; 119:33).

6. Prayer has power to open our eyes to behold wondrous things out of God's Word (Psa. 119:18). It is wonderful how the Bible opens up to one who looks to God in earnest, believing prayer to interpret it to him. Difficulties vanish, obscure passages become clear as day, and old familiar portions become luminous with new meaning, and living with new power. Prayer will do more than a theological education to make the Bible an open book. Only the man of prayer can understand the Bible.

7. Prayer has power to bring the Holy Spirit in all His blessed power and manifold gracious operations into our hearts and lives. "If ye then, being evil," says Jesus, "know how to give good gifts unto your children: how much more shall your heavenly Father give the Holy Spirit to them that ask him?" (Luke 11:13). It was after the first disciples had "continued . . . in prayer and supplication" (Acts 1:14), that "they were all filled with the Holy Ghost" (Acts 2:4). On another occasion *"when they had prayed,* the place was shaken where they were assembled together; and they were all filled with the Holy Ghost" (Acts 4:31). When Peter and John came down to Samaria and found a company of young converts who had not yet experienced the fullness of the Holy Spirit's power, "they . . . prayed for them, that they might receive the Holy Ghost" (Acts 8:15). "And they received the Holy Ghost" (Acts 8:17). It was in answer to prayer that Paul expected the saints in Ephesus "to be strengthened with might by his Spirit in the inner man" (Eph. 3:16), and that "the God of our Lord Jesus Christ, the Father of glory," would give them "the spirit of wisdom and revelation in the knowledge of him" (Eph. 1:17). It is manifestly prayer that brings

the fullness of the Spirit's power into our hearts and lives. One great reason why so many of us have so little of the Holy Spirit's power in our lives and service is because we spend so little time and thought in prayer. We 'have not, because we ask not.'

Every precious spiritual blessing in our own lives is given by our heavenly Father in answer to true prayer. Prayer promotes our own spiritual growth and our likeness to Christ as almost nothing else can. The more time we spend in real, true prayer, other things being equal, the more we shall grow in likeness to our Master.

One of the saintliest and most Christlike men who ever lived was John Welch, the son-in-law of John Knox, the great Scotch reformer. He is said to have given one-third of his time to prayer, and often to have spent a whole night in prayer. One who knew him well, speaking of him after his departure to be with Christ, said of him: "He was a type of Christ."

Many illustrations could be given of the power of prayer to bring our lives into conformity with Christ's. In prayer we gaze into the face of God, and "beholding as in a mirror the glory of the Lord, are transformed into the same image from glory to glory" (II Cor. 3:18, R.V.).

8. But prayer has not only power to promote our own spiritual growth into the likeness of Christ; prayer has also power to bring the fullness of God's power into our work. When the apostolic church saw themselves confronted by obstacles that they could not surmount, "they lifted up their voice to God with one accord" (Acts 4:24). "And when they had prayed," the power came that swept all obstacles before it (Acts 4:31-33; 5:14).

Do you desire the power of God in your Sunday School class, in your personal work, in your preaching, in your training of your children? Pray for it. Hold on to God until you get it. "Men ought always to pray, and not to faint" (Luke 18:1).

I shall never forget a sight I once witnessed. A woman of limited experience in public speaking was called upon to address an audience filling the old Tremont Temple in Boston. It was a notable audience in its make-up as well as in numbers. Many of the leading clergymen of all evangelical denominations were there, also many men prominent in philanthropic and political affairs. As the woman spoke, the audience was hushed, swayed, melted, and molded. Tears coursed down cheeks unwonted to them. The impression made upon many was not only salutary, but permanent. It was an address of marvelous power. The secret of it all lay in the fact, known only to a few, that that woman had spent the whole of the previous night on her face before God in prayer.

It is related of John Livingstone that he spent a night with a few like-minded in prayer and religious converse. On the next day he preached in the Kirk of Shotts with such power that five hundred persons dated their conversion or some definite uplift in their spiritual life from that sermon.

A mother once came to me in great distress about her boy, one of the most incorrigible children I ever knew. "What shall I do?" she cried. "Pray." She did with a new definiteness and earnestness and faith. The change came soon, if not immediately, and the change continues to this day. We can all have power in our work, if we will only believe God's promises regarding prayer, and meet the conditions of prevailing prayer, and lay hold upon God with an importunity, a holy boldness, that will not take no for an answer.

9. But the man of prayer cannot only have power in his own life and service; he can have power in the life and service of others. Prayer has power to bring salvation to others. "If any man see his brother sin a sin which is not unto death, he shall ask, and he shall give him life for them that sin not unto death" (I John 5:16). Prayer avails for the salvation of others where every effort for their salvation fails. There is little doubt

that Saul of Tarsus, the most dangerous human enemy the church of Christ ever had, became Paul the apostle in answer to prayer. There have been countless instances where men and women seemingly past all hope have been converted in most direct and unmistakable answer to prayer.

Prayer will bring blessing upon a church. It will settle church quarrels, allay misunderstandings, root out heresy and bring down gracious revivals from God.

Dr. Spencer tells, in his *Pastor's Sketches,* how a great revival was brought down upon his church by the prayers of a godly old man who was shut up in his room by lameness. In Philadelphia during the pastorate of Dr. Thomas Skinner, three men of God came together in his study to pray. "They literally wrestled in prayer." From this meeting sprang up a powerful revival in that city. One of the most notable, widespread and enduring revivals ever known in this land, according to the account given by Mr. Finney, arose from the prayers of a humble woman who had never seen a revival, but was led to lay hold of God for this.

One of the greatest needs of the hour is that some of God's children should devote themselves to calling upon God until He visits this land again with a mighty outpouring of His Spirit. There have been in times past great revivals without very much preaching, and with almost no machinery. There has never been a great and true revival without much prayer. Many modern so-called revivals are gotten up by man's machinery. Genuine revivals are brought down by prayer.

Prayer will bring wisdom and power to ministers of the Gospel. Paul was a matchless preacher and worker, but he so deeply felt the need of the prayers of God's people, that he asked for them from every church to which he wrote save one (the backslidden church in Galatia). It has been demonstrated again and again that prayer can transform a poor preacher into a good one. If you are not satisfied with your pastor, pray for him. Keep on praying for him and you will soon have a better minister. If you think your present minister a pretty good one, you can make him far better by more prayer. Little do many Christians realize how much they have to do with the powerful or powerless preaching their pastor gives them by their prayer or neglect of prayer.

But the power of prayer reaches across the sea and around the earth. We can contribute to the conversion of the heathen and the evangelization of the world by our prayers. The prayers of believers in America have brought down the power of the Spirit in India and China. Doubtless more men and more money are needed for foreign mission work, but the greatest need of foreign mission work is prayer. It is a sad fact that much money given to foreign mission work has been largely wasted. There has not been enough intelligent prayer back of the giving.

There is mighty power in prayer. It has much to do with our obtaining fullness of power in Christian life and service. The one who will not take time for prayer may as well resign all hope of obtaining the fullness of power God has for him. It is "they that wait upon the Lord" who "shall renew their strength" (Isa. 40:31). Waiting upon the Lord means something more than spending a few minutes at the beginning and close of each day running through some stereotyped form of request. "WAIT UPON THE LORD." True prayer takes time and thought, but it is the great timesaver. At all events, if we are to know fullness of power, we must be men and women of prayer.

CHAPTER V

The Power of a Surrendered Life

"*POWER BELONGETH unto God*," but there is one condition upon which that power is bestowed upon us. That condition is absolute surrender to Him. In Romans 6:13, we read,

> "*Neither yield ye your members as instruments of unrighteousness unto sin: but yield yourselves unto God, as those that are alive from the dead, and your members as instruments of righteousness unto God.*"

Again in Romans 6:22, we read,

> "*But now being made free from sin, and become servants to God, ye have your fruit unto holiness, and the end everlasting life.*"

The great secret of blessedness and power is found in these verses. "*Yield yourselves unto God*"—the whole secret is found in those words. The word translated "yield" in the A.V. is rendered "present" in the R.V. It means, to put at one's disposal. "Put yourselves at God's disposal" is the thought. In other words, surrender yourselves absolutely to God, to be His property, for Him to do with you what He will, and use you as He will. That is the wisest thing anyone can do with himself. By that act he has secured all the blessedness that is possible to man, and day by day, and year by year, it will be bestowed upon him in ever-increasing measure.

If anyone asks, "What is the one thing for me to do if I wish to know all that God has for me?," the answer is very simple. Surrender absolutely to God; say to Him, "Heavenly Father, henceforth I have no will of my own; Thy will be done in me, through me, by me, and regarding me, in all things. I put myself unreservedly in Thy hands; now do with me just what Thou wilt." When one does that, God, who is infinite love, and infinite wisdom, and infinite power, does the very best thing with that one. We may not see at once that it is the best thing, but it is, and sooner or later it will be seen. Sooner or later God floods the heart of him who surrenders absolutely to Him with light, and joy, and fills his life with power. Absolute surrender to God is the secret of blessedness and power. Let us look at some of the things that are definitely said in the Bible to come from absolute surrender.

1. The first of these you will find in John 7:17, R.V.:

"If any man willeth to do his will, he shall know of the teaching. . . ."

Knowledge of the truth comes with the surrender of the will. Nothing so clears the spiritual vision as surrender to the will of God. "God is light, and in him is no darkness at all" (I John 1:5). Surrender to Him opens our eyes to the light which He Himself is. It brings us at once into harmony with all truth. Nothing so blinds the spiritual vision as self-will or sin. I have seen questions which bothered men for years solved in a very short time when those men simply surrendered to God. What was dark as night before has become as light as day.

An unsurrendered will lies back of almost all the skepticism in the world. Oh you who are filled with doubts and ques-

tions, would you have certainty instead of doubt? Yield yourselves to God. Oh you who are floundering in the mire, would
you get your feet on the solid rock? Yield yourselves to God.
Oh you who are trying to feel your way in the dark, would
you see your path plain before you? Yield yourselves to God.
The greatest truths, the truths of most significance for time
and for eternity, cannot be learned by mere investigation and
study. They cannot be reasoned out. They must be seen. The
only one who can see them is the one whose eye is cleared by
absolute surrender to God. "If therefore thine eye be single,"
says Jesus, "thy whole body shall be full of light. But if thine
eye be evil, thy whole body shall be full of darkness . . ." (Matt.
6:22, 23). A surrendered life and will is the secret of light
and knowledge. Many a man has confided to me how he was
wandering in the dark, not knowing what he believed, and not
quite sure if he believed anything. To such I have put the
questions: "Will you surrender your will to God? Will you
give yourself up to God, for Him to do what He will with
you?" And not a single one who has done it but has soon
said, "My doubts are gone, my uncertainties have gone, my
darkness is gone. It is all light now."

2. The next result of a surrendered will and life is power
in prayer. The greatest secret of prevailing prayer is that
which John records from his own joyous experience in I John
3:22,

*"And whatsoever we ask, we receive of him, because we
keep his commandments, and do those things that are pleasing in his sight."*

Just note those wonderful words "whatsoever we ask, we
receive of him." Think of it! not one prayer, great or small,
that fails to get what is sought. Then note the reason: "Because we keep his commandments, and do those things that are
pleasing in his sight." A life entirely surrendered to the doing

of God's will as revealed in His Word, and to doing the things that are pleasing in His sight; a life wholly surrendered to God's will and pleasure, a life wholly at God's disposal, this is the secret of prevailing prayer.

Do you ask why you do not get what you ask, why you cannot say like John: "Whatsoever I ask I get"? It is not because he was an apostle and you are just an everyday Christian. It was because he could say, "I keep his commandments, and do those things [and them only] which are pleasing in his sight," and you can't say that. It was because his life was entirely surrendered to God, and yours isn't. There are many people greatly puzzled because their prayers never seem to reach the ear of God, but fall back powerless to the earth. There is no mystery about it. It is because you have not met the one great fundamental condition of prevailing prayer— a surrendered will, a surrendered life. It is when we make God's will ours that He makes our wills His. "Delight thyself also in the Lord; and he shall give thee the desires of thine heart" (Psa. 37:4). Jesus said to the Father, "Thou hearest me always" (John 11:42). But why? "Oh," you say, "because He was His only begotten Son." Not at all, but because Jesus could say, "I came down from heaven, not to do mine own will, but the will of him that sent me" (John 6:38); and again, "My meat is to do the will of him that sent me" (John 4:34); and again, "Lo, I come . . . to do thy will, O God" (Heb. 10:7).

A surrendered will and a surrendered life is the great secret of prevailing prayer. George Mueller, perhaps, stands out as the one man of our generation who, above all others, has wrought things by prayer. Why? Because many years ago he set out to be and do just what God would have him to be and do, and to daily and deeply ponder God's Word, that he might know His will. He yielded himself to God. There is not one of us who cannot become a mighty prince of God if we will do the same thing.

3. The next result of a surrendered will is a heart overflowing with joy. In the face of awful trial and agony through which He was to pass, Jesus said to His disciples:

> *"If ye keep my commandments, ye shall abide in my love; even as I have kept my Father's commandments, and abide in his love. These things have I spoken unto you, that my joy may be in you, and that your joy may be full."*—John 15:10, 11, R.V.

Jesus had found joy in keeping His Father's commandments, by complete surrender to His will, and now, if they would follow on in that path, His joy would be in them, and their joy would be "fulfilled," or filled full. This is the only way to find fullness of joy—complete, unconditional surrender to God. "Yield yourselves unto God." There is no very great measure of joy in a half-hearted Christian life. Many so-called Christians have just enough religion to make them miserable. They can no longer enjoy the world, and they have not entered into the "joy of the Lord." There they stand, deprived of the "leeks and the onions and the garlic" of Egypt, and without the milk and honey and the finest of the wheat of Canaan. That is a wretched place to be in. The way out is simple, absolute surrender to God. Then your joy will be fulfilled.

I have known so many who have entered into this fullness of joy. Sometimes it has been after a great struggle. They were so afraid to yield absolutely to God, so afraid to say: "O God, I put myself unreservedly into thy hands; do with me what you please." They were afraid God would ask some hard thing, afraid God might whisper "China," "India," or "Africa," and sometimes He has. Sometimes there has been what to the world seemed great sacrifice, the giving up of cherished ambitions, the giving up of those dearly loved, the giving up of very much money, perhaps all one had. But there has been joy, joy "fulfilled," joy filled full.

In one case I have in mind there was great pain, as one lay upon his back with a broken leg in a cast, but there was joy, such overflowing joy that the sufferer lay there with dancing eyes and radiant face and throbbing heart shouting, "Glory, glory, glory!"

There is but one way to find that fullness of joy—a surrendered life. A will and life completely surrendered to the God of love will bring joy under all circumstances. In the olden days one who was thus surrendered to God was led out to be burned at the stake, and he threw his arms around the stake and cried out, "Welcome, cross of Christ! Welcome eternal life!"

4. The next result of a surrendered life is Christ manifesting Himself to us. On the night in which Jesus was betrayed, He said to His disciples:

> *"He that hath my commandments, and keepeth them, he it is that loveth me: and he that loveth me shall be loved of my Father, and I will love him, and will manifest myself to him."*—John 14:21.

A surrender of self to Christ brings Christ to us. The full manifestation of Jesus lies, it is true, in that future glad day when "the Lord himself shall descend from heaven with a shout, with the voice of the archangel, and with the trump of God . . ." (I Thess. 4:16). But there is a present manifestation of Jesus to us now, when the Son and the Father come unto us and make their abode with us (John 14:23). He will manifest Himself unto us. "I don't know what that means," some will say. Have you yielded yourself to Him, are you keeping His commandments, not asking which commandment is great and which is small, which is important, and which is unimportant, but only asking which commandment is His, and keeping that? If you are, you will know what it is to have Him manifest Himself unto you, and that is joy. We are told in one place, "Then were the disciples glad, when they saw the Lord" (John 20:20). You will be glad, when you see the Lord, and you will see Him when you go to Him and say: "I surrender my life absolutely to Thee; now show me Thyself."

5. One more result of the surrendered will and life. Peter tells it in Acts 5:32,

". . . *The Holy Ghost, whom God hath given to them that obey him.*"

The surrendered will and life is the great secret of receiving the Holy Ghost. All turns upon this. We may deal with individual sins, and we may cry to God for the filling of the Holy Ghost, but unless there is total surrender to God at the center of our being, unless we yield ourselves to God, nothing is likely to come of it. Oh, how many have longed, and prayed, and agonized that the Holy Spirit might come upon them, but He came not. There was no complete surrender, there was no yielding of self to God. And then they have yielded themselves to God. They have bowed their faces and said: "O God, I yield, I give myself up utterly to Thee. I place myself unreservedly at Thy disposal. I hold nothing back, and I hold back from nothing that Thou biddest," and, as they have bowed, the Holy Ghost has fallen upon them. Perhaps it was with great surging waves of power and joy; perhaps in a gentle calm that stole over their whole being; perhaps in a still small voice that whispered: ". . . If we ask any thing according to his will, he heareth us: And if we know that He hear us, whatsoever we ask, we know that we have the petitions that we desired of him" (I John 5:14, 15). But whatever way He came, He came; and when He came, power came. The great secret of power for God is the Holy Ghost upon us (Acts 1:8). And the great secret of the Holy Ghost coming upon us is the surrendered will, a yielded life. Oh, how wondrous, how blessed, how glorious is the Holy Spirit's power! Will you have it, my brother? Will you have it, my sister? ". . . Yield yourselves unto God, as those that are alive from the dead, and your members as instruments of righteousness unto God" (Rom 6:13). Will you do it? Will you do it now? We have seen in previous chapters the Power of the Word of God, the Power of the Holy Spirit, the Power of Prayer, but the one great condition of obtaining the power of each and all in our own life and service is a surrendered will, a life surrendered absolutely, unreservedly, totally to God. Will you yield?

Oh, how foolish, how utterly foolish, are those who will not yield, or who hesitate to yield themselves unto God! You are robbing yourself of all that makes life really worth living, and that makes eternity rosy and golden with gladness, beauty, and glory. Will you yield today?

For a complete list of books available from the Sword of the Lord, write to Sword of the Lord Publishers, P. O. Box 1099, Murfreesboro, Tennessee 37133.

Bread for Believers

By Dr. Curtis Hutson

Believer is a common word in the day and age in which we live. But do we really understand the meaning of this important word? Dr. Hutson asks, "What Is a Believer?" in the first chapter of his beautiful new book published by the Sword of the Lord. He carefully answers this question for the reader.

From his original question to the close of the book, he covers the subject completely and thoroughly. You will read about the believer's security, commission, criticism, trouble, chastening, need, responsibility, hope, judgment, knowing God's will, and Heaven, the home of the believers.

This volume would be a wonderful gift for any new believer and should be found on the library shelf of every born-again Christian to be used as a refresher course from time to time. The lovely cover first attracts your eye, but the content comes across with power, doctrinal truths, and warm compassion.

Dr. Hutson's messages are as inspiring in print as they are from the pulpits of America. Get this book to enjoy and share with others.

MANUALS

on Soul Winning

The Golden Path to Successful, Personal Soul Winning

By Dr. John R. Rice. There are many leaflets, courses in periodicals, booklets and pamphlets on soul winning, but nothing in print so complete and thorough as this big manual encompassed within the covers of one large book. Tried-and-proven methods and approaches are presented, together with warmhearted challenges and strong, emotional, yet scriptural appeals to Christians to get involved in this most important work. 15, in most cases, lengthy chapters, but with every word loaded! 314 pages.

The Evangelist and His Work

By Dr. Rice. Often referred to as "the dean of American evangelists," Dr. Rice here, in these 15 chapters, both challenges and comes to the defense of evangelists and their preeminent ministry above all other callings. Every young man feeling a call to the ministry of evangelism should get and thoroughly study this manual; likewise every pastor who believes in and uses the ministry of evangelists should read and ponder this volume. It contains a wealth of scriptural information! 273 pages.